Silent Assassin of Your Average Jonny

Silent Assassin of Your Average Jonny

JOHN MCNICOLL

Story Terrace

CONTENTS

12. JONNY'S PROGRESS

111

1. INTRODUCING YOUR AVERAGE JONNY

A negative mind will find fault in everything, and a positive mind will find an opportunity in everything.

Just before we start, I should say, I'm no doctor, professional or scientist. I'm just your average Jonny. So, if you're experiencing serious mental ill health, anxiety or depression, please get professional medical help straightaway... Then come back and read this book!

This book is about my life facing up to mental health issues that took me completely by surprise. I couldn't understand where they came from, or why they hit me. Before I started having mental health issues, I was just a normal Jonny, laughing my way through life, and having some adventures along the way. I grew up with my brother and sister in a good house, in a sociable family. It was a good upbringing; we had lots of holidays, and enjoyed a normal family life. There is no history of mental illness in my family, and there were no sudden changes in my circumstances that pushed me over the brink. But through the years I was struggling, the effects were very real. As it got worse and worse, it felt like it took complete control of my mind – which is really a horrible and scary situation to be in. My life changed drastically, and if I hadn't done something about it, I would not be in a position to write this book. But I did do something, and if you're struggling, you can too. This book is mainly about how I learned to beat my issues. I'll tell you how I recovered, and what I did to help myself. I'll talk you through what got me through the tough times, and what daily changes I made to get back to a happy and positive state of mind.

I struggled in silence for years, too embarrassed to say anything to anyone. Looking back, I really wish I'd spoken to someone a lot sooner than I did, but I felt daft. I was too cool back then to show weakness, so I ended up struggling as it just got worse and worse. Eventually, I got help, and as soon as I did, my life started to turn around for the better. Whatever you're going through, this isn't going to be an overnight fix – it wasn't for me either – but I realised that, with a bit of hard work, and by changing some daily bad habits I was a lot happier and more positive. You can be too. The anxiety faded and the panic attacks grew less frequent until they disappeared. I was also noticing how much more motivated I felt, and I started achieving a lot more. With less negativity and worry in my life, I was enjoying the present and looking forward to the future with new goals. I stopped worrying about the past.

To this day, the things I went through are still a secret from my family and friends. I haven't mentioned any of it. To be honest I think they'll be more shocked to discover I have written a book than what I went through! From a young age, English wasn't my strong point. I got a foundation English grade in my high school exams. Back then, I had a really bad stutter, and by the time I'd managed to ask for a cup of tea, the pot would have been cold. (The stutter still makes an appearance when I'm excited or drunk). I also have a bad swearing habit and don't notice when I am swearing – I've just kept the best examples in this book for you to enjoy! I don't have the best grammar for this project either, but it should all be in good shape by the time you read this.

I kept everything bottled up, but you don't have to. I know how important – and helpful – it is to speak to someone about your problems, whether it's your family, friends, or professionals, whoever you feel most comfortable opening up to. You will feel a lot better just by getting it out there, and you can start the process of getting better step by step. Don't let it stew inside you as it will only get a lot worse (as I know only too well).

Before I started suffering from mental health issues, I was a very outgoing guy that didn't have a care in the world. I was so laid back, had no worries, and enjoyed life to its fullest. I was very uneducated on mental health and didn't understand what it really was, how it affected you, and what the symptoms were until it got a hold of me and basically gave me a full identity crisis. It changed my whole personality. I wasn't as outgoing when I was with my mates, and the worrying started to take over every part of my life. I went from being a normal guy who didn't care or worry about anything and did what he wanted to someone who worried all the time. I started getting panic attacks that ended up getting bigger and more frequent as the days went on. I also suffered from really bad anxiety which got so out of hand that if I hadn't got help, I would have gone off the rails or had a proper breakdown.

Nobody knew what was going on in my mind. From the outside, nobody could tell that there was anything wrong and I didn't want to tell them. So, I went through my life with my clown face on and tried to make out that everything was normal. I was too embarrassed to ever let my guard down and let anyone know the truth. I managed to scrape by without quitting anything because of what was going on. I didn't drop my job or give up on my life. Later, my hypnotist told me that a lot of people end up stopping something because of associating a panic attack with it. For example, if they have a panic attack on a bus, they'll never get on another bus. I forced myself to carry on my normal routine, but it was a very close thing; I know how scary a panic attack is and how the fear of it happening can take over your life. Some people have even left their jobs because of panic attacks; they just can't face the thought of it happening again, and they take the drastic option to quit.

Whatever you're going through, it's very hard for people who haven't experienced something similar to really understand what it is like. It's also very hard to explain to someone what is actually happening, and I think that's why I ended up speaking to a therapist rather than someone I knew. I would have felt too embarrassed and stupid trying to explain it to my family. Fortunately, the therapist knew exactly what was going on with me, and was able to help. Obviously, everyone is different, so I recommend you turn to whichever person you're going to be most comfortable opening up to.

When I started getting bad panic attacks, then anxiety, everything I did turned into a negative. It felt like I was getting the worst possible outcome every time. The worrying and the stress could strike at any time, even in situations where there was no reason to get worked up about. My overactive mind wouldn't shut off, and life was filled with constant worrying and endlessly negative thoughts. Living with negative thoughts popping up in your head all the time is exhausting. It might sound silly, but it's unbelievable just how powerful your mind actually is, and when it takes over - for good or bad - it can feel uncontrollable. When you're constantly stressed, worried, and overthinking, your mind will only remember all those negative thoughts. Then the subconscious part of your mind turns negative too. Without even thinking of something to worry about, your subconscious mind is way ahead of you bringing up negative thoughts without you actually consciously thinking about any. This led to a big knock-on effect of one bad thought leading to another and another in an endless cycle. As I was uneducated on mental health symptoms and how they can affect you, it made me worry even more; I didn't know what was going on in my head! After I eventually spoke to my therapist, they knew exactly what was happening and helped me to understand why it had been getting worse, and most importantly, how I could fix it. They also told me that thousands of people are going through the exact same thing. Like me, you might feel a bit more comfortable knowing others are going through this too. It isn't just you!

Awareness of mental health issues is on the rise, and at the time of writing, nearly one in every four people is suffering with some form of mental health issue. The last few years have been a very challenging and stressful time for everyone around the world as we've experienced a range of difficult issues and situations, including:

- Coronavirus
- Wars
- Environmental crisis and extreme weather
- Recession and work/money worries
- The pressures of social media

The first time I noticed people talking about mental health was all the celebrities and famous people. But when I read about their issues I thought, *okay, they have problems, but they really aren't in the same situation as me or any other normal folk. They have no money worries, the best therapists, personal trainers etc.* I now know mental health affects everyone whether you're a millionaire, celeb, or just your average Jonny. Luxuries, assets and achievements mean nothing when you're going through mental health issues. So yes, they struggle the same as anyone else but their situation is slightly different. So that's when I wanted to find information that was more suited for my situation, and that's why I wanted to do this book: to help people in the same situation as myself.

For me, negativity, worrying, and stress are the three main categories to keep an eye on to make sure they don't start to take over. I wasted a lot of my valuable time not getting help, as at first, I didn't even know what was wrong with me. Then I wasted more time not knowing where to find help and information. But things changed quickly after I started learning a bit about what I was going through. I read some books by famous people that really helped me start to get better, and I'll go into more detail later in the book. But to begin with, I didn't know anything about mental health, all I had were questions:

- What is mental ill health?
- How does it creep up on us and take over our lives?
- How does your mind work?
- Where do you get help?
- How can you help yourself?
- How can the right and wrong thoughts change your life?
- How is it all linked?

I am going to try and answer all of these questions for you with reference to my experience, to make it all easier to understand, and hopefully speed up the time for you to go get help and start making positive progress. But first, who was I before my mental health issues crept up on me…?

Key points

- Don't suffer in silence, speak to someone – anyone – about what you're going through.
- Do remember, it might be hard for someone to understand what you're going through if they haven't experienced what you've experienced. But also remember that everyone has difficulties in life, and your friends and family want to help you.
- We live in stressful times, but the good news is that awareness of mental health issues is rising all the time, and that makes it easier to find someone to help you, or even just someone who will listen to you without prejudice.
- If you don't want to speak to someone you know, find a therapist or a counsellor, or your GP.
- Even if you're struggling in the depths of depression, or suffering from anxiety, you can do something about it – and I'm living proof – you can get better.

Positive thoughts

- Growth can be painful, change can be painful, but nothing is as painful as staying stuck somewhere you don't belong.
- Your mind believes in what you tell it.
- Focus on the outcome, not the obstacle.

2. POSITIVE JONNY

Push yourself because no one else is going to do it for you.

Before my life started to change for the worse, I was a confident, loud, and laid-back guy. I was very outgoing and always up to something, winding people up, and being a bit of a pain in the arse. They used to call me Coco (like the clown). One of my rugby coaches said to me, 'If you played as much as you fucked about, you would be our best player.' But I laughed it off. Back then, I didn't worry about a thing, except enjoying myself. When I reached 16-18 years old, I started to get distracted by girls and nights out. The 10:00 am rugby match on a Sunday morning wasn't that enjoyable after a Saturday night out, so I ended up kicking rugby into touch. At the time, I thought I was the big man, but looking back I probably wasn't quite as cool as I thought.

By 18 years old, I was bored of Glasgow and the same routine: working all week to go out all weekend to the same places and spending all my money. Yes, the weekends were brilliant, and always a laugh, but I needed more. Without really thinking about it, and without even planning anything, I booked flights for one month in Thailand, followed by a flight to New Zealand for 11 months with a working visa. A year travelling the world on my first adventure, all by myself... What could possibly go wrong?!

I was so relaxed about it all that two days away from leaving, I hadn't packed a single thing, and I didn't even have a backpack. When the big day arrived, I said bye to the family, checked in at the airport, and went for a pint. En route to the bar, I bought a *Lonely Planet* guide for both countries. That was as far as my planning went.

Back then we didn't have mobile phones, easy access to Google, or social media to help us search for places of interest or make travel plans. Throughout my trip, I had to buy phone cards for public phones to stay in touch with my family in Scotland. (Skype was starting to be more widely used by the end of my travels.) Nowadays, you can pretty much organise your full trip on your phone, sitting in your living room. But the fact that I didn't know where I would end up excited me. I'm sure there will be a few of the young team reading this thinking *how the fuck did you live without phones, internet and social media* but it actually felt like a more sociable world back then.

First destination: Bangkok (Thailand). I grabbed my recently-acquired backpack, jumped in a taxi, and headed for Khoasan Road. Driving through the city I was amazed at how busy it was, nothing like Glasgow. Thousands of motorbikes, tuk tuks, and taxis all swinging about from lane to lane with the constant noise of everyone's horns going off. I hadn't been abroad much before that and had not experienced such a big and busy city. The taxi dropped me at Khoasan Road (where 90% of travellers start their Thai adventure) and it was like an explosion of sound, heat and noise. Coming out of a typical Glasgow winter – scraping the ice of the windscreen every morning – to the heat and humidity of Thailand was such a contrast. The place was electric- the markets, bars and food vendors everywhere, with blasting music coming from all the different bars. The smells of all the spices in the street food being made around me were heavy in the air. For the next four days, I visited as much as I could, I partied and tried as much street food as I could manage.

After that, I took an overnight bus and boat over to the islands. The paradise of Kao Ping Kan and all the neighbouring islands are famous for scuba diving, partying, and beaches, and known the world over for the James Bond film *The Man with the Golden Gun* and the Leonardo DiCaprio film, *The Beach*. I spent the rest of my time investigating the islands by scooter, snorkelling, partying, and chilling at the beaches. I always liked martial arts so booked myself into a week's Muay Thai boxing training camp. I didn't have any experience but was soon being put through my paces. What an experience! I learnt so much, and my cardio fitness hit a level I never knew it could reach. To end the week, the professional fighters who taught me took me to the stadium to watch how the real fighters do it. The Thai guys and girls are famous for being on a different level of fitness and toughness, and the atmosphere was crazy. They were like fighting machines, kicking, elbowing, punching, and using their knees. I remember watching a 10-year-old in the ring, confident and smiling, in front of hundreds of people. He didn't look nervous at all. At 10 years old I was shitting myself about going to the dentist and had to be 'encouraged' to sit still with a lollipop. I learned a lot that week and still train in

Muay Thai boxing as a hobby. Thailand is really an amazing place; the people, culture, food and scenery are all incredible. Even when I was leaving, I knew I would go back and it is still my favourite place to visit.

The Thai whiskey had a lot to answer for though! After partying far too much, I ended up arriving in New Zealand for 11 months with just £400 in the account. I think I might have kicked the arse out of it slightly, but never mind. Within a week, I was staying in a big hostel in Christchurch and working as a labourer. Throughout the 11 months, I worked hard, travelled and partied. One day I noticed a job advert for a chef in a place called Mount Cook. This is one place everyone should visit if they get the chance. I wasn't a chef but I could put together a decent meal. After I started cooking, they knew I wasn't another Gordon Ramsay! But I was a hard worker. Between washing the dishes, prepping the food, and gradually getting trained up on the other dishes I was soon in the swing of things. The family took me in and really looked after me while I was there. On my days off I was mountain climbing, living in wee huts around the mountains, ice climbing, kayaking on the melted glacier water, or taking helicopter rides up over the mountains. It was the kind of adventure I was looking for. If you're ever in New Zealand, Mount Cook should definitely be on your to-see list. It's breathtaking, pop into the old mountaineer's café for some local knowledge and food.

For my next adventure, I decided to try dairy farming partly because it was really well-paid. I told the farmer I had a bit of experience which was a lot of shite, but I thought, *how hard can it be*?! Flung in at the deep end, with 500 cows to be milked every day, I quickly realised I was wrong; I didn't have the farming touch. I'm not sure the cows liked me that much either! I was shat on constantly and kicked countless times as I tried to put the sucker thing on the teats. Maybe my technique was causing a bit of a nipple tweak... nothing worse than a bit of nipple tweak! My farming career lasted a whole eight days. I continued travelling around New Zealand, and then ended my trip with an 18,000 ft skydive over the mountains, what a buzz.

Over the next few years, I continued to work hard, party hard, and I travelled all around the world at any opportunity. I got hooked on scuba diving, swimming among all the fish, corals, shipwrecks, and scary-looking creatures. Every dive was different, and I started to see sharks, whales, snakes, rays, sea horses, turtles and loads more. I travelled around Honduras and Guatemala in Central America for 10 weeks scuba diving, volunteering on different projects and travelling about. The only problem I had was I didn't speak any Spanish, and with my Scottish accent, most people didn't understand my English. Never mind, if there's a will there's a way.

While in Honduras I visited a wee island full of diving resorts and reggae bars serving the local dark rum. It was in that cool, mad place that I met this old guy from North America, and his story stuck with me. He explained that he'd had a very stressful job. When it was good, it was very good, but when it was bad, it was terrible. With very big highs and even lower lows, stuck in the rat race chasing the money, spending a fortune keeping up with everyone's expectations and lavish lifestyles, he was constantly worried about the future and couldn't enjoy the present. The worries and stress caused his marriage to fall apart. Then a year later he had a big heart scare caused by the stress of his busy life. After that, he started suffering really bad anxiety about his health, money and future. He realised he wasn't even enjoying his life and knew he needed to change before it was too late. He told me how he had sold everything, taken a leap of faith, quit his job and now lived a stress-free life on a nice big boat. Away from the rat race and all the stress and pressure, his physical health was in a much better place, as well as his mental health. He had learned to enjoy the present. That was the first time I had heard about mental health issues and didn't really understand them until years later when I was in a similar situation.

He also told me how over the years he'd got to know the local people of a wee island that live their lives with no money, electricity, technology, or tourists. Living off the land and sea, they lived simply, but well. I was fascinated and knew I had to visit them. Two days later, I made a big hamper of goodies that would be useful to them. They agreed I could stay a few nights with them and would look after me. My new friend dropped me off on the island and picked me up a few days later.

It was unbelievable. There were no big buildings, no cars and no technology. There were loads of wee huts where they all lived, small canoe-like boats that they carved out of trees and wee happy dogs running about. It was the best experience I have ever had. The people cooked all my meals, took me on jungle treks and showed me all the local wildlife. To be sitting on a beautiful beach watching the local kids diving into the sea with no regard for fashion, no money worries, no technology, just enjoying each other's company and enjoying life was eye-opening; such a different way of living to us. Both nights they shared their homemade alcohol... the bottle was full of roots and leaves, I'm not sure what was actually in it, but it was the strongest bevvy I have ever had! I was sleeping soundly by 8 pm both nights.

In normal life, I was working as a pipe fitter on building sites, usually working away from home and sharing B&Bs with other workers. We used to go out drinking at night and people used to tell me, 'You could be making three times as much money on an oil rig – and you'd only be working half the year.' (It's three weeks on and three weeks off.) So I applied, did my helicopter survival training and in a couple of years I was working on the oil rigs in the North Sea. I was single at the time, so it was the perfect lifestyle for me. As soon as the chopper landed after another three-week stint, I was booking more cheap flights all over the world. Back then I didn't have any worries, I was confident and I enjoyed myself to the fullest. I didn't care what people had to say about me; sometimes other people's input can upset your plans, but I'd already learned not to take any notice of anyone's negative input. If you ever feel bored, stuck in rut or just need your own time, get on a flight to somewhere and experience something new. Getting away from the same usual shit really opens your eyes to different ideas and different ways of life. With the internet to help, it couldn't be easier to do a bit of travelling these days. If you're struggling with the thought of going on your own, consider volunteering somewhere wherever you're going and that will help you to meet people as soon as you arrive.

I did have a few bad experiences while travelling: lost luggage, missed flights, cow shits and extreme mosquito bites, but one of the worst situations was in Bali, on the diving paradise of Gili Trawangan island. We all jumped and made our way down to 30 metres below the surface and I started getting pains in my stomach. I'd had food poisoning loads of times in my travels, but this was very bad timing. For about 20 minutes I don't remember seeing a single fish, I was just concentrating on not shitting myself. I was actually sweating under the water, and in the end, I had no choice... I had to hang back to make sure all the other divers got in front of me (especially the ones with the cameras). Luckily that day I was only wearing my shorts and diving equipment and not a full wetsuit, or it could have been an even shittier situation. Thankfully I got away with it. I relaxed and let everything happen, the fish got a free lunch and I enjoyed the second part of the dive. Based on what I learned later, it's likely that I had a panic attack under there, but on that occasion, I was too busy stopping myself from shitting my pants under the sea to let it get the better of me.

So, from a young age I worked hard, played harder, and enjoyed myself to the fullest. I was independent, fearless and used to turning up in a new country with no idea of what to expect and no understanding of the language. But none of it fazed me. And yet, it was around that time that I started to worry, panic and overthink everything. I started to feel completely different for no reason, as *something* gradually took over my thinking. I couldn't understand what was happening to me. Why was it happening? What was wrong with me? After everything I'd encountered and survived in my life, it didn't make sense. I was getting more upset, annoyed, and completely confused. I now know that I'm not alone; anyone can be affected by panic, anxiety, depression and more, even if it looks like there's no outward reason for it. (You can bet that there will be a lot of people you know quietly going through similar issues).

Over the years, as it got worse and worse, causing more issues and more bad habits, it changed my whole mindset and outlook on life. My feelings changed and my whole approach to life changed for the worse. All my issues were linked:

- Stress
- Anxiety
- Panic attacks
- Overworking mind with negative mindset/unhelpful thoughts

One of the problems is that it starts taking over so gradually that you probably won't even notice it happening until the effects of it are really hitting you hard. And that just makes it harder to get the help you need soon enough. The good news is that even after I got to the stage of letting it creep up on me to the extent that I was nearly floored by it, I still managed to sort it all out. In the next chapters, I'll tell you where it all started to go wrong...

Key points

- Mental health issues can happen to anyone – at any time. I was your average Jonny, enjoying my life, with no idea that I was going to suffer with anxiety and panic attacks.
- When they started, the panic attacks caught up on me so gradually that I didn't know what was happening to me.
- Over time, my whole mindset changed, and my outlook got more and more negative.
- I couldn't understand how I could travel around the world without a care, and yet, the negative feelings I started having completely floored me.

Positive thoughts

- Life is simple, we make it complicated by overthinking and overanalysing.
- Don't wait, the time will never be right. Take action now.
- Make happiness a priority.

3. THE FIRST SIGNS

There is nothing in this world that can trouble you more than your own thoughts.

Growing up I was so busy that I didn't notice how gradually my thoughts and outlook on life were starting to change. But now I look back, I can see how it started; I can see the anxiety and panic attacks creeping up on me. I think because I never stopped and acknowledged the problems to myself, I never thought twice about it. If I experienced feelings of stress, I would make up an excuse for why it happened, then move on. I just wish I'd known some of what I know now. I wish I'd trained my mind at an earlier age, and then everything might have been very different. But at least I can hope that if you're reading this and you've been feeling these negative thoughts creeping up on you, then maybe you can learn from my experiences.

The first time that I experienced what I now understand to be a panic attack was when I was about 17 or 18 years old. I was driving through town on a Saturday morning, and I started to get really bad heartburn. I have had heartburn loads of times, but this was different, and a lot worse. I then started to get a shortness of breath as if I couldn't get a good enough breath in. Between the heartburn and shortness of breath, I started to panic a wee bit, as I'd never experienced anything like that before. I knew that any breathing problems are usually classed as urgent, so when I got home I (stupidly) Googled the symptoms, and the next thing I knew, I was on my way to A&E, thinking I was in a really bad way. (Don't Google medical issues!) As I sat nervously in the waiting room with all the other people whose Friday nights had obviously got a bit out of hand and ended up in there with their injuries, my thoughts were in overdrive and the panic kept bubbling up. Eventually, a nurse called me in, checked my pulse and heart rate, and carried out some other checks. Everything came back showing that I was absolutely fine, everything was in good working order. All I had was acid reflux and although it's worse than heartburn, it was nothing to worry about. All of that panic for the want of some strong heartburn medication, and a Google prognosis that I was about to die.

Looking back at it – and I didn't notice this at the time – the shortness of breath, tightness of chest, and worry all stopped after I was told there was nothing wrong with me. I thought they'd all been part of one big medical issue I was having. When you struggle with anxiety or have a panic attack, the bad symptoms all stop after it wears off, and your body is still in good working order, proving there is nothing to worry about. That's easy to say, but when you get all the horrible feelings happening at once and taking over your thinking, it's even easier to panic. So, that was my first (reasonably small) panic attack, I just didn't know it.

The feelings hit me in most areas of my life. I could be doing all sorts of normal things - things I'd done a hundred times before - and still get a surge of anxiety or a panic attack. But there were always other things that I could blame it on. For example, after nights out I would feel horrendous, full of worry, feelings of panic, and depression. For ages, I just blamed it on the drink. Alcohol is a depressant, and after a big night out, you're 100% going to feel like shit because it slows down the processes in your brain and nervous system. In the short term, you might feel more relaxed and happy as it is a fast short-term fix, but after it wears off, it will leave you more depressed, worried and generally feeling shit. If you have mental health issues, alcohol isn't a long-term fix and will only ever make matters worse. (More on this later.) Over the last few years, I have spoken to loads of people that have struggled with different problems, and every one of them hit the drink looking for short-term relief from their problems but ended up in a much worse situation in the end, where they were more worried, crippled by depression, or got to the point where they couldn't leave the house without a drink. What starts out as a short-term fix turns into something that you will chase constantly.

It is normal for everyone in the world to feel a bit anxious from time to time. It is a normal response from your body if you're worried or uptight about something coming up. Maybe an exam, an interview, or an important occasion. But after those things have passed, you know that the symptoms will die down. If you feel your anxiety is becoming more and more common, or even constant, and affecting your day, or stopping you from sleeping at night, don't ignore it. Because if you do, it will only keep getting worse. The sooner you catch it, the easier it is to turn it around. The best thing to do is get help, talk to someone, and get that process of recovery started. It's nothing to be worried or embarrassed about. Like my therapist told me on day one, from time to time your mind just gets a bit lost or gets stuck in overthinking things, and then that can spiral out of control if you let it. It just needs to be reprogrammed and updated on what it should be working on. Just like your phone and computer, every now and then you need to update your mind and give it a wee reset or a mental MOT!

Key points

- It isn't always easy to see how it starts, and it's only when I look back that I'm able to see the tell-tale signs of anxiety creeping up on me.
- My first panic attack felt like a very physical illness; some of the symptoms were a bit like a heart attack.
- Watch out for anxiety and negative feelings creeping up on you. It's like getting into a bath that's being filled with hot water; it's easy to go on coping until you realise the bath is too hot. The sooner you can understand what's happening, the sooner you can get out without being burned!
- It can be easy to put your anxiety, negative thinking, or depression down to other things. You might be feeling anxious because of work, or pressures at home, but if it gets to the point where the anxiety is taking over your life, you might need to give your mind a bit of an MOT.

Positive thoughts

- The quality of your life is a direct reflection of the quality of your thoughts, beliefs, habits and perspective.

- When you focus on the good, the good gets better.
- Results happen over time, not overnight. Work hard, stay positive, and be patient.

4. WHAT ARE MENTAL HEALTH PROBLEMS?

A negative mind will never give you a positive life.

So, what are we actually talking about when we speak of mental health problems? There are loads of different conditions like addiction, anger issues, anxiety, depression, eating disorders, OCD, panic attacks, paranoia, phobias, suicidal thoughts, trauma-related issues, and many more. Let's look at some of them in more detail:

Depression

What do we mean when we talk about depression?

Depression is a mood disorder that causes a persistent feeling of sadness, negativity, and loss of interest. It affects how you feel, think, and behave, causing emotional and physical problems. It will cause problems with your attention and memory, as well as your information processing and decision-making. Signs of depression could include:

- Persistent feelings of sadness
- Loss of interest in things
- Trouble sleeping or over-sleeping
- Changes in appetite, weight change

- Decreased energy
- Feeling worthless, useless, and lonely
- Difficultly thinking clearly
- Frustration
- Physical aches and pains
- Recurrent negative thoughts
- Thoughts of death and suicide
- Anger
- Isolation

Generally, depression is not a result of a single event and may be a result of a mix of events and factors. The longer you leave it, the worse the thoughts, emotions, and feelings will get. Sometimes people who struggle to deal with their thoughts, feelings, and emotions can struggle with their mental health. And everyone who suffers with mental health issues will have their own unique issues and experiences. But I know from taking action that getting professional help to change your daily bad habits can change the outcome of your day – and your life – making difficulties easier to deal with, and helping you to feel a lot more positive.

Anxiety and the fight or flight response

Anxiety is a feeling of worry or fear that something bad is going to happen. It can affect your thoughts, emotions, and, as I know only too well, it can bring physical symptoms too, like a pounding heart, sweating and shortness of breath. That's because our body is preparing us to fight or run away. It's called the fight or flight response, and it comes from caveman days. Back then, the stresses in life were a bit different. You didn't have to worry about keeping your job or paying your gas bill, but you did have to worry about running into a man-eating animal. If you did, your body would respond by producing lots of adrenaline ready for you to fight for your life or run away.

So, it's worth knowing that anxiety is actually a normal human response to potentially dangerous or harmful situations. We still feel that same response to stress, but instead of sabretooth tigers and life-or-death situations, we've got other things to worry about. Most people will get anxious in certain situations throughout their life; it could be taking exams that gets your anxiety going, giving a speech, going on a date, or going to the dentist (I used to be guilty of that one, as I'll tell you later). People can get anxious just thinking about doing one of those things.

Feeling anxious in any of those situations is perfectly normal, and after the event or the thought has passed, your anxiety levels will drop back to their standard level and you'll feel relaxed and normal again. In some situations, anxiety can even be a positive thing. It can help you to perform better in sports or might make you feel sharper or more alert in an exam.

The problem with stress now is that we still get that massive surge of adrenaline in response to situations and events that aren't life-threatening. It could be something as simple as running late to meet your girlfriend, or getting stuck in traffic, but when the anxiety kicks in, you still get a massive surge of adrenaline that you don't need. We all have so many stressful situations in our lives now that we're bombarded by fight-or-flight responses we don't need.

People who have an anxiety disorder feel all of those symptoms of anxiety more than they should. It's like a car alarm that keeps going off for no reason. You can't just hope the problem will go away; you might need to get some professional help to fix your alarm (or your response to anxiety).

If the anxiety doesn't go away, it can – and probably will – worsen over time, to the point that it will interfere with your daily life. And when I say 'interfere' that can mean anything from stopping you from doing certain things, right through to stopping you from leaving the house. Don't underestimate its power, anxiety can be devastating, and it can take over your mind and body very fast, unless you get help, or find ways of addressing it yourself. There are loads of different symptoms of anxiety, some of the most common symptoms include:

- Catastrophising (fearing the worst possible outcome for every event)
- Fear and feelings of dread
- Feeling tense
- Negative thinking
- Nervousness
- Overthinking
- Panic
- Paranoia
- Trouble focusing or making decisions
- Worrying excessively

It can also cause physical symptoms, including:

- Increased heart rate
- Rapid breathing
- Sweating
- Tiredness, fatigue, and weakness
- Twitches

When suffering with bad anxiety, a silly little issue can escalate in your head causing so much worry and self-recrimination for no reason at all. If you've ever felt like that, you'll know how hard it can be to move on from it afterwards. Leave it like I did – and the feelings will only get bottled up and can escalate into even more mental health issues, like panic attacks and depression. But the better news is that it is easy to stop your mind from being swamped by over-the-top thoughts and emotions. So, the big question is: when should you get help?

As soon as you feel your anxiety is affecting your daily thoughts, emotions, and activities, you should reach out for the help you need. Anxiety can be treated in different ways at different stages, but as with everything else, the sooner you start – before it starts taking over your life – the better. People with anxiety tend to overthink and worry excessively about everything. Some people live with the fight or flight response symptoms running constantly throughout the day. (That is exhausting.) But by reprogramming your mind to a more confident, positive mindset, you can stop the anxiety from creeping in and taking over. You don't need to learn to stop the negative thoughts, it's actually much more effective for you to take control of them. Bit by bit you can master those thoughts and show them who's in charge of your mind! I'll give you some tips on how to do that later.

Panic attacks

Panic attacks are related to anxiety. A panic attack is like a brief episode of intense anxiety with physical symptoms. This can happen for no apparent reason at any time. You may experience an overwhelming sense of fear, apprehension, and anxiety as well as loads of different physical symptoms all at once making it feel absolutely overpowering and scary. The physical symptoms of a panic attack may include:

- Chills/hot flashes,
- Distress
- Excessive sweating
- Numbness
- Shortness of breath
- Tensed up muscles
- Tight chest, and/or accelerated heart rate and breathing, which may be accompanied by chest pains.
- Trembling, dizziness, nausea, sickness

It's a very scary experience when a panic attack comes on. The physical symptoms can be similar to serious heart problems, and that can make you panic even more. As well as all the physical symptoms, your mind goes into overdrive with worry and panic. And worse still, a panic attack can happen at any time, for no apparent reason. In my experience, they can last from just a few minutes up to 20 minutes. After you have a panic attack in a certain situation, your mind will pair the situation and the response, making it increasingly likely that you'll have other panic attacks when you're in the same situation in the future.

As I know well, panic attacks can be very frightening and intense, but it's important for you to know that they are not dangerous. It doesn't cause any physical harm, and after the symptoms have died down your body will be back to full working order with no issues. But that doesn't mean you should settle for living your life with panic attacks. The likelihood is that having had one, more will follow. For me, they went on getting more frequent and stronger until it felt like they were taking over my life. Don't let that happen to you; if you are having attacks, go and see your GP and/or find a good therapist straightaway. The earlier you step in and take control, the easier it is to put a stop to them and train your mind to override them and prevent them from coming on.

As I struggled most with bad anxiety and panic attacks, I can only really explain what I went through with them. But as so many mental health conditions are linked – and may be caused by a negative thought, experience or feeling – the way to help yourself is often the same or similar. As the saying goes, 'thoughts become things.' If you can control your negative thoughts and feelings and change them to more positive ones, you will be in a much better place.

It has been suggested that some mental ill health is caused by chemical imbalances in the brain, but there is no single cause for mental health problems. You may experience difficulties after a bad life experience, experiencing a trauma (or the after-effects of childhood trauma), experiencing ill health or medical conditions, stress, loneliness, money worries, the effects of drugs and alcohol, or even finding yourself stuck in a situation you're unable to get out of. There are so many things that can set it off.

Eating disorders

One of the commonest mental health issues of our time is the range of eating disorders. This is a mental health condition where you use the control of food to cope with feelings and other situations. Anyone can get an eating disorder but it is much more common among teenagers these days. The disorder causes people to fixate on their weight and what they look like, leading them to obsess over what they eat, giving them an unhealthy attitude to food. Eating disorders can take over your life, making you dangerously under or overweight. Signs and symptoms of an eating disorder can include:

- Constant worry about appearance and weight
- Avoiding socialising when food is involved
- Deliberately being sick / taking laxatives
- Exercising too much
- Mood issues
- Feeling unhappy/depressed
- Body insecurity (body image issues)
- Reliance on fat burners and slimming pills

Eating disorders and mental health illnesses commonly occur together with anxiety and depression. With the pressure of society, social media, and sporting culture, eating disorders (alongside mental health issues) are on the rise at an alarming rate.

It wasn't like that in my day. When I left school at 16 years old, no one spoke about mental health or training your mind. Nowadays, it is a lot different. I thought I was doing a pretty good job of looking after myself, working very hard, training very hard in the gym, travelling, and watching my diet; I thought I was in a strong place. Yes, I was fit and strong, but I didn't look after my mind the way I should have. I didn't know how to. I did very little to make sure my mindset was just as strong as my body, and I did nothing to preserve a positive outlook. There are other benefits of taking the same approach to your mental health as your physical health; when you exercise your mind, you will have much better memory, concentration, focus and determination, and you'll be able to control your thoughts better. If you look at all the best athletes in the world, so much of their success is down to their mindset; sometimes their mindset is stronger even than their physical body. Without that focus, your mind will give up well before your body will. Your mind plays tricks on you to make you give up, but you can train yourself to push through these negative thoughts and not give up with excuses; you can push on. Here are some examples of how that works:

Example 1: Going for a jog

You're all organised to go for a jog. You're feeling up for it, and you're looking forward to it. You know you can do it – you've done it before – but ten minutes in, your mind starts speaking up with all the excuses: *I'm not feeling it today. I need a drink of water. Let's stop for two minutes. My legs are sore. Fuck it, it let's just walk the rest.* Deep down, you know you're fit enough to complete the run, but your mind tries anything and everything to stop you. If you're able to ignore what your mind is telling you, you'll complete that jog, and feel much better about yourself.

In sporting events between two equal contenders, the person with the stronger mindset will be more focused, and they'll feel better able to keep going without quitting, giving them a competitive edge. Martial arts is a good example. The competitor with the stronger mindset will almost always come out on top. Back in the day when Conor McGregor was coming up the ranks in mixed martial arts on the UFC, it was his hunger for success, combined with a cast iron focus and a powerful mindset that took him to the top. He knew he had won every fight before he even walked into the cage. He also played tricks on his opponents' mindsets, making them doubt themselves. That's how powerful the mind really is. Check out some of his interesting documentaries about his attention to mindset, focus, and concentration.

Example 2: Exam coming up

You have an exam in a week's time. You know you're pretty organised and ready for it, but for that whole week, you're a worrying wreck. All the negative energy and thoughts of failure put you in a panic. Then you start thinking you're going to fail. With a week to go, why do we get so worked up and drive ourselves crazy with bad and unhelpful thoughts? Until we walk in there and see the questions, how do we know we are going to fail before the exam day? Most of the time, we'll leave the exam room and realise it wasn't all that bad. That week of stress and worry only affected our studying time and ruined our sleep! Try giving yourself a different perspective. Some people use positive mantras to help them feel better about their chances. Some people visualise walking into the exam room feeling calm and confident.

Example 3: Absolutely knackered but can't sleep

All day at work you're so tired, struggling to keep your eyes open, looking forward to getting home and going straight to bed. Then the time comes and you're buzzing to jump in bed, but just as you close your eyes it's like someone turned a light on in your head. Your brain won't switch off and silly thoughts pop up and keep your mind whirring. You've been knackered all day, just waiting for sleep, and now you're wide awake. When I was going through a bad spell, I struggled really badly to get to sleep some nights while my mind was going into overdrive. The more you try the more annoyed you get. If you're struggling to get to sleep, pay some attention to your sleep hygiene. Turn off your phone a good half hour before bed, and get into the habit of going to bed at the same time, and going through the same rituals so that your mind understands what is going on and starts pumping out those sleep hormones!

Key points

- Depression is a mood disorder that causes a range of negative feelings and can be the result of many factors.
- Anxiety is the feeling that something bad is going to happen. It can cause physical symptoms as a result of the increased adrenaline in your body (the fight or flight response).
- Anxiety is a normal response to stress, but it can go into overdrive in response to everyday things.
- Panic attacks are a physical manifestation of anxiety causing a range of symptoms, from shortness of breath to heart palpitations.
- The body will go back to normal after a panic attack, but it is still a very scary and intense experience that can last for many minutes.
- Eating disorders are one of the most common mental health issues of our times, ranging from under-eating issues like bulimia and anorexia to over-eating.
- Developing the right kind of mindset is critical in beating mental health issues and overcoming the negative messages your mind can send you.

Positive thoughts

- Do not give your past the power to define your future.
- Stay away from negative people; they have a problem for every solution.
- Fear kills more dreams than failure ever will.

5. THOUGHTS BECOME THINGS

Your mind will believe in what you tell it, so tell it positive things.

So where does my mental health story start?

It was Hogmanay, (31st of December for those of you who don't know!) and I was heading out with my girlfriend to celebrate at a big street party. We started to get into the party spirit with a few drinks and we were already drunk before we headed out. The next thing we both knew, we were waking up in our hotel room. Neither of us felt rough, but we couldn't remember anything after the first few hours of the party. While having breakfast we noticed one of the pictures on our phone from 11:00, right outside our hotel, just before we'd collapsed in our room. We had kicked the arse out of the night and never even made it to the bells or the fireworks. Oh well, we'd saved a bit of money and got a great sleep, so we checked out, got lunch and headed home. I was driving, and we were about an hour and a half into our journey home when, all of sudden, I started to feel my chest getting all tight. I was struggling to get a good breath of oxygen in. Instead of my normal breathing pattern, I was taking big breaths in, faster and faster, and I felt my fingers going numb, like the pins and needles feeling. I started to panic, what the fuck was going on?

The more I sat there thinking about it, the worse it got. I could feel myself overheating, sweat was running down my back and my face. I opened the window for some fresh air to cool me down and my girlfriend could see that I didn't look too good. By then, my body was tense, my chest was tight, and I was numb and struggling to breathe. I told her I was fine, but she knew I wasn't anything like 100%. We pulled over so she could drive, and by the time we'd switched seats, most of my symptoms had worn off. I was an emotional wreck inside, my head going mad. *What the fuck just happened? What's wrong with me? Do I need a doctor? When will it happen again?* Eventually, I fell asleep and woke up not far from the house, but after that, I couldn't get it out of my head. It was terrifying just how fast the symptoms came on.

We were due to meet her family in a local pub for new year and I was going to drive so everyone could get home easier later. As we arrived everyone was well on enjoying themselves, but after what had happened, I was struggling to relax. I felt so stressed about it all on the way back from the toilet I swung by the bar and ordered a few drinks to take my mind off it all. The rest of the night was fine, but I knew it wasn't the end of it. That day was the start of the silent assassin taking over. After that experience, I never mentioned it to anyone and when my girlfriend asked, I just blamed the drink. Because it happened in the car, the thoughts and feelings of that bad experience popped up again every time I got back in the car, leaving me thinking, *Is it going to happen again?* Back then I didn't know anything about panic attacks. When I was driving, I was more worried that I wouldn't be able to control it and that anyone else in the car would notice something was wrong with me. I was completely confused by it all, not just worrying if it would happen again, but thinking, *Will it be worse next time?*

Over the next few years, my anxiety and panic attacks started to creep into different situations, trying to take over everything I did. And when it happened in a new situation or scenario, I knew that every time after that, it was likely to happen again, always getting stronger and more uncomfortable. It sounds really stupid trying to explain it, but when you're struggling with all the symptoms it's very hard to just ignore it. Experiencing tight pains in your chest, struggling to breathe, feeling all your muscles tense up, experiencing numbness, and overheating so you can't stop sweating are all scary feelings that would send most people hurrying to A&E, like I had that first time. It doesn't matter how many times it happens, you panic and your mind goes into overdrive every single time, making it worse. It is really fucking horrible. Being in that same situation again and knowing the same thing could happen again at any time is scary. Even if you have done something a thousand times before and nothing has happened, you still think, *this could be the day it happens again.*

On some level, I realised that if I could take my mind off it before it got out of control, it wouldn't hit me so hard. I started eating sweets when I was driving, or phoned people for a chat to distract my mind. I think I put over a stone of weight on dipping into my constant stash of Skittles, Haribo and wine gums! Throughout all this, I still managed to hide it all from my family and friends. Why did I carry on keeping it quiet? I think it was because I was known for not caring, having a laugh and getting up to no good; I didn't want people to see me any other way.

By then, my girlfriend was pregnant, and I used that as an excuse to have a drink at any social event, because she was driving. Sometimes, I just had a drink to relax in case I had another attack. Throughout that period, I would get good days and bad days. I could go four-to-five days without an attack, but then it would happen again, and knowing that it could creep up at any time was a constant worry. I still worked offshore then and flying back and forward on the helicopters never bothered me. It was a long trip out, a bit boring, and noisy; but it never worried me, until one day... I had a really big panic attack lasting 10-15 minutes on the helicopter heading offshore. It was the worst so far with my emotions surging, and my mind going at 100mph while stuck in a big dry suit and life jacket. Because it was so intense I knew then that every time I got on a chopper it was going to happen again, with the possibility that it would escalate out of control. I would even start to worry about it the night before knowing it was going to happen. It was the worst situation I ever got in It wasn't like driving or other situations, I couldn't distract myself with eating, music, or conversation. When you're in a helicopter, there is nothing to distract you from your thoughts and feelings. It's far too noisy to chat with the other boys, and you're just sitting there for an hour and a half with nothing to do. It's so easy for your mind to go fucking nuts! I had never been bothered about flying; I'd even jumped out of a helicopter, so why was it causing me so much pain now?

My son was due a month later, and I started to overthink that and worry about the big day. I kept thinking *what happens if I have a panic attack in there while my girlfriend is giving birth?* Can you imagine that? Me being there to help, and I end up having a panic attack, and passing out in a bed next to her?! I would never have heard the end of that one. It's funny now looking back, but I was actually really worried about it all. On the day, I remembered there were a few beers in the boot, just in case I needed them, but I was actually far too busy to worry about anything. Just as well as I don't think it would have gone down too well: 'Do you mind taking five while I nip out for a quick beer?'

Battered by constant worry, negative thoughts, and relentless overthinking, my self-confidence started to take a big hit. I'd gone from being an over-the-top, centre-of-attention kind of guy to a quiet, worrying, overthinking guy. Even though no one noticed, I knew I couldn't keep going like that or my confidence would dip further and affect my personal and professional life even more. It's hard to live a normal life when you don't know what's going to set off another attack. On another occasion, I was going through airport security and started having a panic attack while queuing up to go through the scanners and get searched. As I got through Strathclyde, the two of them were pulling random people over, asking them questions and looking at travel plans. I could see them both looking at me which wasn't helping. I must have looked really dodgy – a young guy by himself, covered in tattoos, looking tense and sweaty. They must have thought I was smuggling a bag of drugs down my pants. No wonder I was shouted over.

The final straw was when it started affecting me when I was working out. Throughout everything I'd endured, working out in the gym or Muay Thai boxing was the one thing helping me to feel good about myself. I had just finished a 10k run on the treadmill, but suddenly became very dizzy, and felt extremely out of breath. I had to sit down; I felt completely drained even though I'd done the run easily enough. It was really getting to me, every time the anxiety took something over it made me even more angry and upset. I knew that I was always fine after the attack passed, so I wasn't worried about my health. It was more the intensity of the attacks that worried me and the dreadful feeling that they were going to keep happening. Even writing this now, it sounds ridiculous that I didn't do something about it sooner. Why did I leave it for so long, letting it take over every part of my life? Partly it's because it all happens so very fast, and before you know it, your life's been taken over. I know people that have quit their jobs, stopped going out and abandoned their hobbies in case they somehow trigger it again. I didn't quit anything, even when my anxiety was at its worst, but was very close; the helicopters were the big issue for me. If I hadn't been able to get on the helicopter, it would have cost me my job.

I knew I couldn't keep going and eventually booked an appointment with my GP, still not knowing what the fuck was wrong with me. After describing what I was going through, I was told I was having bad panic attacks and prescribed some medication designed to relax me and calm my overthinking mind. I noticed a massive difference on the medication and for the next few months, I was in a much better place. I would still worry about having an attack and could sometimes feel one coming on, but it never led anywhere. What a difference I felt. I had a stash of the pills everywhere; I wouldn't leave the house without them. It was such a huge relief knowing that I could start to enjoy myself a bit more.

But the overthinking didn't stop, and the worrying continued. Even with a massive weight off my shoulders, I knew it was only a short-term fix. I didn't think I could (or should) rely on the pills all my life, and it still hadn't fixed the problem of my overactive negative thinking. For the next three to four months, my life was easier, and some sense of normality returned, but I knew I had to start looking at a long-term fix.

Everyone will experience anxiety and panic at some point in their lives, like if you're starting a new job, going for an interview, giving a speech, or waiting for medical news. But then, after the situation has passed, you'll be back to normal. However, some people can't control their worries and thoughts. Their anxiety is more constant and can affect their daily life, as mine did. If you feel you're worried, overthinking, or struggling to switch off, and it is starting to affect your daily life, go and see your GP. If only I'd done that sooner, it would have saved me a lot of pain later on.

Key points

- When it came on suddenly, I didn't realise that the sweating and tightness in my chest and difficulty breathing was a sign of a panic attack.
- At the time, I didn't discuss my experience of anxiety and panic attacks with anybody; I wish that I had talked to someone about it all much sooner.
- Once you have had one panic attack in a certain situation, you get conditioned into thinking it will happen again.
- I realised that I could distract my mind in certain situations (e.g. driving) by eating sweets, but it wasn't a proper solution.
- The constant worry took a big toll on my confidence, and seeing my GP was the first step in tackling the issue.

Positive thoughts

- Once you replace negative thoughts with positive thoughts, you will get positive results.
- Success takes time, stay focused and be patient.
- Accept your past without regrets, handle your present with confidence, face your future without fear.

6. BAWBAG HAS ARRIVED!

Don't ruin a good day today by thinking about a shit yesterday.

The pills helped, but I knew I couldn't keep relying on them. I did some research online. The sheer quantity of information was a bit overwhelming at first, but there is a lot of good information available online and on social media. Reading about people's lived experiences of dealing with anxiety, panic attacks and other issues can be really helpful. But you have to be careful; a lot of the information I read on one site would be contradicted on the next site, and you have to sift through a few young insta-bloggers or whatever they're called, trying to tell everyone how to live their lives even though they look about twelve years old, and they're probably living in their mum's attic!

Throughout my research, hypnosis kept coming up. I remembered that I'd had hypnosis years ago – a cheap online deal to stop smoking. I could have known back then that I shouldn't have expected too much from a cheap, bargain deal. I went in and the lady explained she would relax me into a comfortable state, that I might even fall asleep, but that she would be working on my mind throughout, to help me stop smoking. It sounded great, I'd tried for years and never managed to give up. I was there for an hour, listening to her annoying voice, rabbiting on and on. The whole time I was there I was thinking, *when is she going to shut up so I can go and have a cigarette?* So that wasn't very successful. I've also seen a show on holiday where people were getting hypnotised and running about the stage thinking they were a chicken. So, I wasn't too confident in the idea of hypnosis. I kept dismissing it, but as my research continued, the idea of it kept popping up again. In the end, I thought *fuck it, what can possibly go wrong?* I made some enquiries and booked a free consultation so I could get a sense of how it would work and then make my mind up. But I thought *if I get the feeling I'm going to be turned into a chicken and run about the office, I'll not be back!*

Turning up not quite knowing what to expect, I was quite surprised at how relaxing it all felt. There was music on, a diffuser with a strong scent of ginger and lavender, and a big comfy chair. We spoke for a while about what I was going through and about mental health, with regard to how the mind works, and how it's all connected. He explained how the mind is so powerful and in control of everything you do daily, but sometimes gets confused when trying to help or warn you, and can actually work against you. Your mind will believe what you tell it – for good and bad – and over time, if you're able to change what you tell your mind, your thoughts and feelings will change.

He explained how a panic attack can occur when the fight or flight response is triggered in your brain, even when there is no real danger about to happen. Your body thinks it's helping to look after you, but really it's doing the opposite. Once it happens once it will go on happening because your mind believes it is helping you get ready to face some danger or threat. People are brought up worrying about everything these days, so it is easy for an overreacting mindset to spiral out of control. The stimulus is different for everyone, it might be a bad experience or an unhappy memory, but for me, it was years of worry, negativity and an overworking mind. Hypnosis is very good for relaxing your body and reprogramming your mind, changing those negative thoughts to positive ones.

This isn't an overnight fix, but if you engage in the hypnosis and put the extra work in, I think any issue is fixable. I also recommend that you have a recording of your sessions to listen to. I listened to my recordings when I went to bed every night to top up the effects of the hypnosis. It really helped me, and it will help you too. As you get used to it, the sounds of the session starting will relax you and that's perfect - any work on the mind is more effective when you're in such a relaxed state. The messages from the session will keep filtering through to your unconscious mind.

Even in that very first session, I learned more in that 45 mins than in months of researching. It helped me to understand what was happening to me, why it started, and most importantly, how I had the power to change it. I actually felt that I was in a better place, just by understanding everything that was happening to me.

In my first appointment, the hypnotist explained it is impossible for your body to have a panic attack if you can control your thoughts. When you have an attack, you worry more, which makes the attack feel stronger. But then when it wears off, all the symptoms stop, and your body is in good working order, proving that your body is fine and it's just your mind worrying far too much, causing the feelings and the panic to escalate. If you distract your mind as soon as you feel a panic attack coming on it won't come to anything.

We decided to make a wee joke of my anxiety to take the sting out of it, so I decided to call it Bawbag. A good Glaswegian word used all the time when slagging someone off. I have also been called a Bawbag millions of times myself. So, whenever I felt it trying to kick off again, I needed to make a point of stopping and saying 'Right, here comes Bawbag again,' then do a breathing exercise:

Breathe in for 4 seconds
Hold your breath for 4 seconds
Breathe out for 4 seconds

Keep counting, and repeat the exercise until the feelings pass. Doing this distracts you from your negative thoughts, and also slows your breathing down, which slows your heart rate down, which stops your body from getting flooded with oxygen.

To be honest, I fell asleep at every one of my hypnosis appointments, but that's fine as your subconscious mind is still taking in the information throughout the session. After six appointments, once every two weeks, doing my exercises, and listening to my sleep recording, I started to see big changes. Sometimes I wasn't sure, but then I would do something and realise that I was doing it without any problems; the anxiety didn't surge, and the panic attacks didn't come. Even though I was using the pills less and less, I felt more relaxed and positive, and my mind had stopped going into overdrive. I found that I was able to distract my mind more easily, preventing anything from coming on. It got to the point where I had my pills with me all the time but wasn't using them. Before I knew it, I was driving, working out, working and socialising with no attacks or pills. Eventually, I was only using the pills on my helicopter rides to work and back. And then, a few months after I started the hypnosis, I realised I hadn't had a panic attack in months. Yes, I still had good and bad days, but I was prepared for the bad days, and any time I felt the start of a Bawbag arriving, I could diffuse the situation before it came to anything.

Eventually, I was completely finished with the pills and stopped taking them around with me. The difference in me was unbelievable. After all that time struggling and feeling too worried to speak out, I was in a much better place for getting help. Just understanding what was happening, and knowing that it wasn't a medical issue was reassuring. If only I'd known a bit of basic information on it all at the start, it would never have escalated. The mind is very powerful and can take over your life if you let it. Obviously, my issues weren't anywhere near as bad as other people that are struggling, but it's all quite similar or linked. When you're in a horrible mindset with negative thoughts and feelings you're not actually thinking clearly. That's why it's so important to speak out about what's going on for you and get help as soon as you can. After eight months of getting help, doing my exercises and changing the bad habits I'd fallen into, the panic attacks had gone away, and I was so much more positive and enjoying my life, worry-free. The combination of medicine first, followed by the hypnosis – combined with the exercises – worked for me. I would definitely recommend booking a free consultation for yourself and making up your own mind. But before you do that, in the next chapter we'll take a deeper look at hypnosis and the mind.

Key points

- Hypnosis isn't a short-term fix, but over time, the positive messages filtered through to my unconscious mind and helped me to diffuse difficult situations.
- Understanding more about what had been happening to me also helped me to feel a bit better; I knew that I wasn't physically sick and that I could get over my anxiety issues.
- Breathing exercises are an effective way of combating a panic attack.
- For me, the medicine-first approach followed by hypnosis really worked.

Positive thoughts

- Little by little, day by day, what is meant for you will come to be.
- Excuses make today easy, but they make tomorrow hard. Discipline makes today harder, but makes tomorrow easy.
- Nobody can make you happy until you are happy with yourself first

7. HYPNOSIS AND THE MIND

Stop being afraid of what can go wrong, be excited about what could go right.

So, what is hypnosis therapy?

Hypnosis therapy is a type of mind-body intervention in which hypnosis is used to create a state of focused attention and increased suggestibility to help treat a medical or psychological disorder or concern.

Hypnosis allows you to be more open to suggestions and more receptive to making a healthful change in your perceptions, sensations, emotions, memories, thoughts and behaviours. To be hypnotised, you have to be relaxed, and it helps if you enter into the process with an open mind. If you fight it or resist it, then it may not work for you. The first time I went in, I did fight it a bit, thinking *this isn't going to work.* Thankfully, I proved to be very susceptible, and even though I was fighting it a little bit, it worked. After that first appointment, I trusted the therapist and was a lot more relaxed and focused on what he was saying, which helped me to get the full benefit from my sessions. Also, you're paying for it, so you're only wasting your money if you go in fighting it. Just let your therapist help you.

Hypnosis can be helpful in addressing a wide range of issues, including:

- Addictions
- Allergies
- Anger management
- Anxiety
- Beating bad habits
- Bed wetting
- Blushing
- Confidence
- Depression
- Fear of flying
- Irritable bowel syndrome
- Insomnia
- Memory enhancements
- Negativity
- Obsessive-compulsive disorder
- Overthinking/rumination
- Migraines
- Panic attacks
- Phobias
- Self-doubt and self-belief issues
- Sleep disorder
- Stopping smoking

There are loads more things hypnosis can help with; the police have even used it to solve murders in the past.

I can almost guarantee that everyone reading this has been in a hypnotic state brought on by themselves, without even knowing. When you go into a trance-like state in which you have a heightened focus and concentration, you probably don't even notice it. Young kids can get into that state very easily with their incredible imaginations when they're playing. It does get a bit harder as we get older, but see if you can notice the times when it happens to you. For example:

Driving your car: when you're driving on a familiar road, you fall into a wee dream state and before you know it, you have driven five miles without even noticing. You were able to drive safely, watch out for dangers, and keep the car going the right way even though your mind was relaxed and elsewhere.

Waking up and sleeping: just before we drift off to sleep or as you're going from sleep to wakefulness, your mind is in a more receptive state, and this is why therapists get you in this state to reinforce the helpful suggestions your subconscious mind needs to hear.

Watching a film: when you're watching a film you can get so absorbed in it that you actually feel like you are there. Young kids can go in and out of this state playing with their toys or watching TV. When they're in that space, you could shout their name or wave chocolate at them and they wouldn't hear or notice you.

This is the exact state where your mind will take in new information and is most receptive to reprogramming. You might think *this sounds like a lot of shite*! Trust me, before going through it myself, I wouldn't have believed some of it myself, but now I have gone through it, and I know how it all works, I find it pretty interesting.

When you focus on problems you have more problems. When you focus on possibilities, you have more opportunities.

The deeper you get into it, the more you learn about the mind. People talk about neuroplasticity – which describes just how much you can reprogramme your mind. You don't need to know a lot about that to know that your mind is very open to suggestion. Here are the basics:

The subconscious mind is like a tape player, until you change the tape it will not change its thoughts. (I feel old mentioning a tape player; most of the young team won't even have seen one.) Once your subconscious mind accepts an idea (bad or good), it begins to execute it. It can't tell the difference between what is real and imagined. With over 6,000 thoughts a day, your mind will only remember the ones that stand out, which in most cases are the stressful and negative ones.

Repetitive thoughts that are repeated often enough will eventually become fixed in the subconscious mind. And then they'll just pop up whether you want to think about those things or not. Have you had a time when you had a bad thought or experience, and the thoughts around it keep popping up in your head? Then you would think to yourself, *why the fuck am I thinking about this again?* Then it keeps on popping up.

The conscious mind is the part of your mind where you are aware of your thoughts and decisions. By contrast, the subconscious is the part of the mind that makes decisions without us needing to actively think about them. The subconscious makes up to 95% of your brain power and handles everything your body needs to function without consciously thinking about it, like breathing, walking, eating and making memories. It's like a massive memory bank for all the memories, emotions and beliefs about everything. That is why it's so powerful and can affect your thoughts, emotions and outcomes. It's like a computer or phone operating system and sometimes it just needs updating or reprogramming to get it back to full working order.

I mentioned fight or flight earlier – where a person's body responds to stress in a certain way by preparing the limbs for action in case you need to face up to or escape a dangerous situation. You could stand and fight, run away or completely freeze. Everyone is different and acts differently in stressful situations. People with anxiety can get locked in this state so that their bodies are always on alert, causing worry, fear, and eventually exhaustion. Living like that takes it out of you! The imbalance can be caused by a negative thought process that keeps activating the fight or flight response. Your subconscious mind responds to this as normal and automatically puts you on alert.

You can see how an overactive mind can cause all sorts of anxiety and panic attacks, and how the fight or flight response keeps the mind and body in a state of high alert. I didn't know any of this at the beginning of my journey and left it late before I got help and found out what was really happening. Hopefully, anyone reading this might understand it all a bit better and get help sooner to stop it from spiralling out of control.

Key points

- Hypnosis describes a state of intense attention which can lead to someone being more receptive to taking helpful ideas on board.
- You need to be receptive and open to the idea that hypnosis can help you.
- You have probably already experienced a state of deep intense concentration – like a hypnotic state – without even realising it.
- Your mind can get stuck in negative thinking patterns, but you have the power to embed more positive messages in your mind.

Positive thoughts

- Kindness will take you further than hatred ever will.
- It's hard to beat a person who never gives up.
- Don't let the bad days, make you think you have a bad life.

8. HOLY SHIT! IT GOT WORSE...

If you're having a bad day, remember someone is dating your ex and thinking they got lucky! Smile.

For the next few years, I had a great mindset and was living life to the fullest again, anxiety and panic-attack-free. I was enjoying family life and bringing our son up. I was making good money and started up another business. I'd just about finished the work in our family home that we'd bought and renovated. Life couldn't have got any better. After everything I'd been through, I'd sorted sort myself out and the bad days were behind me. It wouldn't come back, and even if it did, it couldn't be any worse than it had been before.

But then coronavirus happened, and everything turned to shit. This was a really horrible time for everyone in the world, and our family were very lucky in that we didn't have any deaths due to covid. As my job offshore involved working in small, cramped areas with others, sharing rooms on the platform and huddling together in the chopper, if anyone caught covid, the whole rig would have had it in days. So for the majority of covid, I was jobless, and had no money coming in. All the years of sticking spare money into different stocks and shares accounts and watching them grow couldn't save me; within a few weeks, the whole market crashed on its arse. All my shares were worth absolutely nothing and that was money that would have been very useful at the time. It also got challenging bringing up our first child, constantly being stuck in the house.

Dealing with everything that was going on and not being able to get away from it put a big strain on my relationship with my partner. Times were getting harder, with the whole world at a standstill as it dealt with this natural disaster. Having spent a lot of time and money on it, I had no choice but to fold my other business and take a big hit. Everything was slowly falling apart. Our relationship was struggling too, and I moved out of the house. The hardest thing about that was not being around my kid 24/7. I missed being in the family house for him waking up every morning. So, after a year of getting our family home perfect, I was back at my parents' house. Then, a month later, I was driving home and crashed my car; it was a complete write-off. Everything was building up on me and I could feel the stress mounting. In the space of just six months, I experienced just about every stressful thing you can imagine:

- Money worries
- Relationship issues
- Business failures
- Work uncertainties
- Stocks and shares crash
- Car crash
- Loss of independence
- Losing daily access to my kid and the family home
- The uncertainty of the future

My head was completely fucked with it all. It felt like everything I had worked and saved for just fell apart in such a short time. I was really uptight and stressed, my head was going crazy and my anxiety was getting worse. Some nights I couldn't get to sleep because my mind couldn't switch off; it was going at 100 mph with all my issues going round and round. Throughout the whole time, with everything going on, I was training hard in the garden or gym as that was the only time my mind would turn off from the big clusterfuck that was my life. It was a massive stress relief that helped take my mind off everything else and made me feel temporarily better after I'd done a hard workout. And then, just to add to everything else, I ripped the tendon between my rotary cuff and bicep. So I was unable to train, and with that one release gone, my motivation started to drop, healthy eating went out the window, and I felt horrible. It really is amazing how good you can feel after a workout and eating healthily, but I was going in the opposite direction. I was eating shit and lazing about at night, staying up late watching rubbish on TV. I felt horrendous, my energy was gone and I was just ruminating on all my issues. Then I'd get up late and repeat the same pattern the next day, feeling like shit from the moment I woke up. Within 10 seconds of waking, all the worries and thoughts were back, getting more ingrained and more intense every day. The only time I wasn't thinking about all the problems around me was when I was playing with my child. When I was with him, I could put on my best game face and pretend that nothing was wrong, laughing at it all, but really my head was going absolutely out of control, not knowing how the fuck I was going to get out of the shit.

For a while, I just tried to take each day as it came, trying to blank out all my worries and uncertainties. But although I was getting through the day, I wasn't moving forward at all. One afternoon I saw an advert on social media for Tyson Fury's new book, *Behind the Mask*. I have always been a fan of 'the big man' and I thought it would help take my mind off it all. What a brilliant book it was: I finished it in two days. It's incredible what he went through to become the heavyweight world champion, and even more incredible that the big, tough fighter was brought so low with bad mental health issues, even becoming suicidal. While everyone thought Fury was just having fun and going off the rails after becoming world champion, he was secretly suffering. It shows anyone can get affected by mental health issues and his story shows how serious it can really get. For him to sort himself out and then become world champion again shows you the measure of the man. But of all the brave things he's done, one of the bravest was opening up on it all in his book to try and help others.

I knew I needed to change my daily habits and my mindset before I lost the plot. The longer I left it, the more intense it got. Along with the lack of sleep, the endless cycle of negative and worrying thoughts was just piling on the pain. It is easy to say now, but back then it was really hard to see past all the troubles I was having. Reading that book gave me the kick up the arse I needed to get help and motivate myself again. That week I started to sort myself out. Yes, I had some pretty serious life issues. Yes, I'd had a bit of bad luck but I still had my health and my family; I still had a future. Shit happens, but there's a time to stop feeling sorry for yourself and make changes. One thing I do know – nothing is ever going to get any better if you just sit about doing fuck all!

Ever since I had hypnosis for my panic attacks, I haven't had another one. Not even when I was going through that rubbish period in my life. So I thought hypnosis would be a good start on this occasion too. Like the last time, it helped to relax my overactive mind. And there were really useful exercises to help me deal with the unwanted thoughts popping up all the time. People that have bad anxiety can have unwanted thoughts popping up 24/7 and struggle to get rid of them as they escalate out of control. These exercises work especially well alongside hypnosis but you can try them too, whether you're seeing a hypnotist or not.

What I'm about to say might sound really daft, but it honestly works. Every time a bad thought enters your head and you notice it, make a point of stopping it in its tracks and tell your mind, 'This thought isn't helpful right now, and I don't want it coming up any more.' Or 'Fuck off, you're not helping.' (You can vary what you say to suit you.) Do it every time the thought pops up again. Don't let it get away with it. If you put 100% into doing this it's amazing how well it works. Yes, I know it sounds fucking stupid, but by making it known that you don't want this thought appearing in your mind, you'll also start to notice what thoughts are popping up and how regularly. That will help you be more alert to all the unhelpful thoughts; you might be surprised by just how many you have in a day. Of course, we all get unhelpful thoughts from time to time, but it's when you get stuck into a pattern of believing them that you have problems. One word of advice: say the words in your head, not out loud or you might get some funny looks standing in Asda! Every time you notice this or other unhelpful thoughts, cut them off. Try it for yourself, don't give up, and I think you'll notice how easy it is to cut off the unwanted thoughts that constantly pop up out of your head.

Between the hypnosis, more recordings to listen to at night, and the exercises to help me stop my negative thoughts from taking over, I was heading in the right direction. I started to eat better, started light training at the gym, and stopped sitting up watching rubbish on TV. I started to feel better and more motivated to sort out the problems in my life that had hit me all at once. Instead of wasting my free time scrolling through social media, I went for big walks and really benefitted from the fresh air and daylight. While I was walking, I listened to podcasts and books on Audible, learning and training the mind as I walked. I could feel the changes happening. The things I'd been really worried about and ruminating on didn't seem quite so important. I realised I could get over all of it; nothing was as big a deal as I'd thought. When you look back, it can be hard to understand why you let something bother you so much, but when you're going through it all when you're hit by one problem after another, it's not so easy to look up and see the light. There's a knock-on effect of bad behaviours: you feel depressed so you stay up late, and try to soothe the pain away with food and drink, but that only ever keeps you trapped in depression. The lack of exercise and lack of daylight, the solitude and the social media, the bad food and alcohol – they're all fuel to a massive fire.

Key points

- You have to keep working on preserving your positive mental health. I thought I was completely better, but a combination of factors made things worse for me.
- When I got into a bad cycle of negative thinking, my motivation dropped, and I got stuck in less positive habits.
- It helped me to read how Tyson Fury overcame his mental health issues; see if there are any books or podcasts out there that can help you.
- A combination of hypnosis, listening to recordings of our hypnosis sessions in bed, and some brain re-training exercises helped me move past my issues.
- Make a point of noticing when bad or unhelpful thoughts enter your head and confront them; this is a really useful way of helping you regain control.

Positive thoughts

- It's the hard days and the times that challenge you to your very core that really determine who you are.
- The struggle you're facing today is developing the strength for tomorrow.
- Falling down is an accident, staying down is a choice.

9. SUGAR, BOOZE AND SOCIAL MEDIA

Remember some things have to end for better things to begin.

I have always been very active and eaten pretty healthily, but it was during that really low point I described in the last chapter that I noticed how much my daily choices and bad habits have a knock-on effect throughout the day and on to the next. That doesn't mean you can't have any fun at all, but if you keep an 'everything in moderation' mindset, it can keep you feeling good and help to maintain a more positive, motivated outlook. If you feel good, you will be happier, more positive and confident and you'll go on to achieve more throughout your day.

When I was low, my daily choices didn't help me at all. Eating shit food, not staying hydrated, bad sleep hygiene, losing hours on social media and binge-watching any old shit, fuelled by too much alcohol: all these behaviours left me feeling tired and deflated. I had no energy and I was lost in a negative mindset, which made the problems I was facing in life feel much worse.

Since improving myself and changing my daily choices I have seen a massive difference in my mental and physical health, and my overall mindset. I started waking up earlier, feeling fresher and more motivated. I would be a lot happier and more positive throughout the day and achieve a lot more. I'd be less affected and more able to cope with minor problems. I'm definitely no health freak or some kind of nutritional expert; I still love a night out, I still have takeaways and I can't have a cup of tea without a family-size bar of chocolate with it! If you're feeling low, I know how easy it is to get a quick fix from sweets, alcohol or comfort food. I know what it's like after a night out, after you've had a skinful and a late night; the last thing you want when you're feeling rough the next morning is a nice healthy salad. No, you reach for the sweets and chocolate and self-soothe with a beer or two and another takeaway. As a short-term fix, it feels good to laze about. But it's a vicious cycle; you get very little good energy from the shit food, and you don't have the get-up-and-go to get out, so you stay lying about on the couch all day. The next day you feel sluggish and tired all over again; that's the knock-on effect of a night out and all the bad choices that follow. Let's look at some of the main culprits in a bit more detail:

Sugar

Sugar activates the same pleasure centres in the brain as cocaine does. When you eat it, feel-good chemicals like dopamine and opioids are released, activating the reward circuit in the brain. It is very addictive and gives you a fast – but short-term – feel-good factor. But the reality is that it can actually cause you to feel down and depressed as it wears off. Because it is such a fast, easy comfort fix for anyone who is feeling a bit low or lethargic, chocolate is one of the first things people reach for. Sugar is a massive issue these days and the obesity epidemic is spreading.

Alcohol and drugs

Drinking and drugs may help people to relax or get a short-term buzz... until they wear off, and then you feel just as bad – if not worse – than you did before. For people with mental health issues, drugs and alcohol can seem like they offer fixes to help them get through a difficult time, take their mind off their worries and relax, but the relief is only ever temporary, which is what causes people to chase those feelings more and more. That's why people get so addicted, to the point where they're unable to cope without taking something to cover their worries and their problems. Anyone trying to mask their problems with alcohol and drugs will only cause more problems, worries and negativity in the long run.

Coffee/stimulant drinks

When I had bad panic attacks and anxiety, I stopped drinking coffee. Caffeine can stimulate your fight or flight responses, so if you're anxious or uptight, coffee is only going to make you feel more worked up. Also, when a coffee wears off it can give you a comedown effect, leaving you feeling low and tired. I also found that when my mind was in overdrive and I was struggling to sleep, I didn't need anything to speed up my thoughts or keep me awake.

Social media and mobile phones

When I was younger, social media didn't exist. To me, the word 'social' meant everyone out and about socialising, enjoying each other's company. I had a great childhood and grew up having a lot of fun. No mobile phones, phone cameras, or social media. We were able to muck about, make mistakes and say what we wanted without having to worry about turning up on someone's social media feed looking like an idiot.

Young people growing up now shouldn't have to worry so much about what people think, and shouldn't have to care about how they look. Kids just need to have fun, make mistakes and learn from it, that's what childhood is about. Nowadays with cameras everywhere, and other people's views and expectations dominating their lives, the younger generations are having to grow up a lot faster. They don't have very long to enjoy being kids.

You see kids in primary school worried about their appearance and getting likes on social media. When I was younger we did a lot of stupid things, and after an embarrassing night out, I'd get slagged for it for a few days, then it would blow over and get forgotten about. Or else the next weekend would arrive and someone else would do something daft and they would take my place. Nowadays, with everyone recording everything, a bad night out could ruin a young person's life if it goes viral. It's just as well that there weren't any camera phones when I was younger. With the states and scrapes I got into, I'd have been an internet superstar for all the wrong reasons.

Young people are under so much pressure with social media, and trying to keep up-to-date with celebrity trends and the latest fashion. They're forced to grow up faster, but unlike my day when we knew how to banter, they're so self-conscious and too worried about other people's opinions. Many of them try to make their social media accounts paint a perfect picture of their life. Photoshopping their image and trying to make themselves look rich and successful, their accounts are full of fake happy selfies. When they got to events, they're more interested in making sure everyone knows they were there. People don't enjoy the present moment, they're too busy trying to get that perfect picture for social media. It's all very strange because social media is the complete opposite of social. It does very little to bring people together. Instead, it causes jealousy, loneliness, worry, fear and depression and fosters addictive behaviours, with people 'doom-scrolling' their lives away.

Years ago, I went on a date with a girl I met on a dating website. She had six pictures on her page, and we spoke for a while. When I went to meet her, she messaged me that she was standing outside her house. I couldn't see her, then I realised I'd driven right past her. She didn't look anything like her pictures, and I'd driven by thinking it was somebody else. Funnily enough, that date didn't turn into a relationship! Nowadays a lot of girls are so self-conscious and so worried about their appearance that they can't leave the house without spending hours in front of the mirror. What would people say if they saw them looking less than perfect?

All the social media apps know exactly what you like, and what you search for, so they'll always bring up similar material to get your attention and keep you on their sites for longer. People are wasting their precious time away scrolling through shite and looking at everyone else's fake happy living-the-dream lifestyle pictures. Most young people will spend more than 4-hours a day achieving nothing or posting pictures to see what likes and comments they receive, just so they get their short-term happy fix.

Social media used in the correct way can be bloody amazing. For keeping up with family and friends, advertising your business, and getting your content out there fast, it's great, and I've made good use of the internet to research new travel destinations. But if you're using it as a boredom fix, it's only going to cause problems for your mindset. I've spent years working offshore, and it can be very boring at times when you're stuck out in the middle of the sea with little to do. It could be quite annoying seeing everyone back at home having fun in all their posts while I was stuck out there working, but I would still scroll through all the notifications, knowing I'd get pissed off seeing what I was missing out on. It's just like when I was in a bad place, and I would laze around looking at everyone else's happy successful pictures even though I knew it made me feel even worse.

In the last few years, mental health issues have skyrocketed at an alarming rate, thanks in part to our obsession with social media. It can affect all ages, but it's especially prominent – and worrying – with the younger generation. They can be so caught up in chasing likes and favourable comments that it can lead to issues like addiction, loneliness, worry, fear, jealousy, depression, negativity, insecurities, unhappiness, paranoia and sleeping issues, not to mention hours of wasted time.

For some people, the reality is that if they post a picture and get 60 likes and 25 nice comments, but also get one bad comment, they'll only remember that one bad comment, and then spend too much time worrying or getting upset over it. More than 75% of people look at their social media as soon as they wake up and last thing at night, before going to sleep. This is a really bad habit to get into. Two reasons why you need to stop this:

1. Phone screen light actually stops the production of serotonin – the natural sleep drug that activates when you turn the lights off and get ready for sleep. With your mind awake, it's harder to get to sleep, and harder to get into a restful deep sleep.

2. Even more important: as you fall asleep and your mind and body relax, your subconscious mind processes the thoughts, feelings and experiences of the day. If you've just spent the last half an hour on your phone feeling pissed off, ungrateful, lonely, or resentful, those thoughts will still be circulating while you sleep. Then, you wake up, grab your phone and top up those thoughts and feelings which will stay with you throughout the day. When you wake up, do you really need to see what everyone else is doing and thinking? Start your day off right and concentrate on yourself. When you stop scrolling, you'll free up enough free time to take up a hobby, or learn something new.

The next time you're out for dinner, or having a night out, have a look around. See how many people are sitting in silence on their phones. I was out having dinner recently and there was a couple on a date at the table next to me, both attached to their phones all night, with a few pictures taken of their food in between courses. Not one bit of conversation or laughter the whole time, they didn't even chat about the food. (Maybe they were sitting there texting each other, I'm not sure.) If that was a special occasion, imagine the atmosphere when they were back at the house.

While my son has been growing up, I do as much as possible with him when I get home from work. I want him to know what a proper father-son relationship feels like. It's unbelievable the number of parents who take their kids to a soft play centre or a park, chuck them in, and sit on social media the whole time, not giving an arse about their kid, and never playing with them. Sad isn't it?

So, the big question is, what do we do about it? How do we get out of the rut, end our dependency on our bad habits and find a new way?

Key points

- The choices you make when you're feeling low only keep the cycle of depression and anxiety rolling.
- From sugar and social media to alcohol and drugs, we all get stuck in patterns of behaviour that only make us feel worse.
- There is intense pressure on us all – particularly young people – to conform to someone else's ideals, all fuelled by social media.

- Chasing likes and continually scrolling on our phones can consume people's every waking moment – and is particularly unhelpful before bed when the screen light can actually stop your sleep hormones from working properly.

Positive thoughts

- Learn from yesterday, live for today, and hope for tomorrow.
- Make the rest of your life, the best of your life.
- It's not how we make mistakes, but how we correct them that defines us.

WE ARE A SAD GENERATION
WITH HAPPY PICTURES

10. THE FEELGOOD FACTOR

Worrying more won't make your life better. Educating yourself, taking calculated risks, and acting more wisely will.

Ready to experience the feel-good factor and break your dependency on bad habits? People who are feeling good and can live with their problems (instead of trying to mask them) will get up feeling positive and get on with their day. While I've been writing this, I've spoken to a lot of people who are going through their own issues and it can be a bit harder for them to get going positively. These wee habits will help you:

Wake up right

As soon as you wake up, get up. Don't snooze or lie about in your bed looking at other people's lives on social media; that will only get your day off to a bad start. It's a massive waste of your time looking at what other people are doing, and before you know it, you'll have wasted an hour or more scrolling endlessly. There's loads of evidence proving just how addictive social media is, and it can really impact your mental health. Wake up and put some feel-good music on if it helps. Jump out of bed and have a shower (cold is better if you can handle it)! Have a good breakfast, and if you can manage it, have a few minutes with a tea or coffee outside. Just getting a bit of fresh air – and some sunshine if you're lucky – will do you the world of good. When you get up in plenty of time, you'll find it's so much easier to get organised and get your head right for the day ahead. Many of us are so used to rushing around like headless chickens first thing in the morning that starting your day in a more laid-back way feels really positive. Every person that I have spoken to with depression, anxiety and other mental health issues feels better for being more organised. A good routine that works for you will help you feel more in control of your day – and your life. Build in whatever feel-good factors will give you the best chance of heading into the day in the right frame of mind. Some people swear by getting out for a walk or run as soon as they get up; some people have a workout or favour some reading time when they wake up. We all have our own little rituals that work for us, and inspire us to start our day off right.

Meditation

A great way to get the day off to a good start, bring it to a restful close, or create some calm in your day is meditation. Mediation can put you in a deep state of relaxation and tranquillity to calm the mind. When you meditate, you focus your attention and eliminate all the jumbled thoughts that you might be struggling to get out of your head, causing you to worry and feel stressed. Meditation can give you a sense of calm, peace and balance. It can be used to help you relax and cope with stress by refocusing your attention on something calming. It can help you learn to stay centred and maintain your inner peace – even if that sounds impossible to you right now! Meditation can feel tricky at first, but there are loads of great apps to help you. Even if you find it difficult to begin with, just setting aside a few minutes to clear your mind is still a great thing to do. It'll give you a little bit of peace in your busy day. Meditation can help you to reduce your anxiety, enhance your mental health and self-awareness and increase concentration, which can in turn lead to reduced memory loss and improved sleep hygiene.

See the light

Try to get as much fresh air and natural light as you can. If you're stuck in an office, sitting about in artificial light, go for a walk at lunchtime; it'll make you feel much better. Some research suggests that too much artificial light (instead of natural light) can cause people to feel depressed. You might have heard of seasonal affective disorder, which is commonly understood as the winter blues, when daylight is so scarce. Grab as much as you can – it's good for your vitamin D levels, which is good for your bones.

Stay active

Have you noticed that if you sit about all day at work or at home, you get tired more easily? You feel like you can't be arsed to do anything. I'm sure there have been times when we've all said, 'I'll go to the gym later,' or 'I'll have that walk tomorrow,' but when later comes and when tomorrow has slipped away, we're still sitting around feeling like all our energy has drained away. On the other hand, you may have noticed that after a busy day of running about, you actually feel more energised and you've still got the energy for a walk or a workout. The best bit is that expending energy and being active helps us combat stress and releases loads of feelgood chemicals too. The double whammy of getting some exercise outside is even more beneficial for us.

Yoga

One of the best ways to stay active is yoga. Yoga is an ancient practice that involves physical poses, concentration and breathing exercises. Throughout a session of yoga, you will promote endurance, strength, flexibility, concentration, calmness and wellbeing. Yoga is very popular worldwide these days and is recommended for helping people going through mental health issues. Because it is a low-impact workout, yoga is a really good way of exercising without putting too big a strain on the body. It has been shown to lower stress levels, and improve your focus while simultaneously increasing endorphins. It's also been suggested that it increases brain gamma-aminobutyric (GABA) levels – the feelgood chemicals help decrease anxiety and improve mood.

Watch what you eat

Try and be organised with your food. Pack a healthy lunch for work to stop you from snacking on junk. Prepare or plan easy, nutritious meals for after work that will actually be easier than a takeaway. (When we remove the excuse to order a takeaway or throw some processed rubbish in the oven, it gets a lot harder to give in to bad habits.) Eating healthily and staying active can become habits too, and the easier you make it to stick to those habits, the more you'll go on keeping them. And

I promise you that when you start seeing – and feeling – the benefits, you'll want to carry on doing them.

Get organised, get a routine

Whether you're struggling with a mental health issue or not, I think that being more organised in your life will help you have a more positive day, achieve more and maintain good daily habits. For me, being organised can be the difference between having a good and bad day. I know how the least wee issue can get blown out of proportion, heaping stress and negativity on your shoulders. But I also know that being prepared and getting organised can make it much likelier that you'll have a positive day with no extra unwanted worries taking over. Here are some ideas on how you can get organised.

Weekly planner

Whether you use an app or an old-school diary, getting all your appointments, classes, and social events down in writing will help you eliminate some stress and get organised for the week ahead.

Eliminate unnecessary stress

You can't control all the stress points in your life, but you can at least do something about all the stressors that are under your control. A great example is being on time. If you're like me, you probably hate rushing to be somewhere. The stress piles up and suddenly everything feels tense and anxious. Make a point to check out your route ahead of time, and try to get into the habit of arriving everywhere a little bit early. It saves the rushing, overthinking and panic and it'll help you feel more relaxed and positive throughout the day.

To-do lists

When people are trying to work through their depression or anxiety, the smallest little things – like getting up and getting clean, staying on top of the housework, and getting out to meet people – can feel like huge obstacles. If you're one of those people who likes making to-do lists and enjoys ticking off your daily tasks, then it will really help you to make a list of daily activities that you can tick off as you go. The trick is to make your list as detailed as you can. Nothing starts the day off better than being able to put a big tick in the box just for getting up and getting a shower, so include anything that feels challenging for you to do on a daily basis. Getting through difficult days one tick at a time can really help you stay on track, stay motivated, and get things done.

Routine

One thing that all of these ideas have in common is routine. You'll probably find that when you start planning your days and weeks and thinking through your daily tasks, you will slip into a routine that works for you, almost without trying. Give some of these ideas a try, and I think you'll find it easier to stay on track and stay focused. It's amazing how the positive effects of a few simple things can accumulate, help to reduce your stresses and make life feel more manageable.

Other people

Don't underestimate the importance of the people surrounding you in life. There is a saying that 'you will turn out the same as the people around you.' If you're surrounded by positive people with successful mindsets, that will brush off on you. Just the same as if you're surrounded by people that are always moaning, lazy, and feeling sorry for themselves, you're going to feel a bit shit. It's like a box of strawberries – if you have a box of strawberries and one of them turns mouldy, all the other strawberries will turn mouldy very quickly. But if you take away the one mouldy strawberry, the others won't be affected. It's the same when you're stuck with people who are negative. I noticed it offshore one trip. We were having a laugh when another guy arrived – a nice enough guy – but he was constantly negative, moaning, disagreeing and finding problems everywhere. It started to affect the team's mood. After a couple of days, I couldn't take anymore; it wasn't just annoying, it was bringing me down with him. After that, I put my earphones in during tea breaks to cancel out his noise. On a related topic: don't be in a hurry to share your ideas for a new business, hobby or project with other people. As Conor McGregor said, don't tell anyone what you're doing until it's done. Outside energy can throw off your goals. People's input can make you doubt yourself, or feel too embarrassed to continue with your plan. Do it, prove it to them and then move on to the next one!

Your personal gurus

I've mentioned Conor McGregor a few times in this book and I really recommend taking what you can from people you respect who have something to say about their own battles with mental health issues and the lessons they follow for living a good life. You'll find your own, but as well as Conor, I'd recommend:

The main man Fury

Tyson Fury really helped me realise what was happening to me and gave me a kick up the arse to start sorting myself out. It was just what I needed. I have always been a big fan of his because of his boxing achievements, and his funny attitude in all his interviews; he knows how to up his opponents. Throughout his career, he has achieved so much to become heavyweight champion of the world. While growing up – and throughout his career – he suffered with mental health issues, struggling more than anyone would have known. He lived two lives in one: the true Tyson going through his problems in secret and Tyson Fury the character – the funny, loud performer everyone knows. Whether you like boxing or not, this man is a fucking legend for his life achievements in sport, and for speaking out about his mental health issues, helping millions around the world in the process. Someone like him – rich and famous, with a hard man reputation to protect – didn't need to open up about his life troubles, but he did it to help others. After Tyson became world champion, his mental health issues nearly drove him to the point of suicide. After a massive high, he went into an equally massive low. Tyson was then stripped of his belts, and went to a very bad place, using drugs and drinks to get by. Going from worse to worse, and at the end of his rope, the big man eventually got help, conquered his demons, got back to training and became world champion for the second time.

His book, *Behind the Mask,* is really good, honest and very helpful for others going through their own issues. Showing that someone who is hard-as-fuck could end up suffering proves that anyone can suffer with mental health issues. It doesn't matter how hard you are, how rich you are or what you have achieved. Given his upbringing and boxing career, Fury let it bottle up inside him, and was afraid of looking weak, but that's what led to him having a major breakdown. It shows the importance of speaking out to someone to get the help you need, whether it's family, a friend, a therapist, or someone on the other end of a helpline. Talking to someone will make a difference and even if it's just small steps at first, it will start the process of getting better. As well as his eye-opening book, there are some really good videos and speeches from Tyson on YouTube, Spotify etc. talking about mental health. He's doing incredible work to help so many others.

Ant Middleton

You will probably know Ant Middleton from the programme *SAS Who Dares Wins,* where members of the public were put through an ordeal similar to special forces training. Ant was in the special forces before this programme and was one of the marshals pushing the contestants to their very limit, causing most of them to give up. A lot of people thought he was loud and disrespectful to the contestants but he was actually pushing them to overcome their fears and complete the task.

Since leaving the show, Ant has helped millions with his books, TV shows, and live speeches on all kinds of mental health topics and motivation to better your life. He has been through a lot himself, suffering with his own issues. It is incredible what Ant has now achieved after everything he went through, and his books: *First Man In, Zero Negativity, The Fear Bubble, The Wall*, and *Mental Fitness* make for fascinating reading.

Ant's books are full of positive mental health advice and motivation, helping readers tap into his positive mindset. I would highly recommend reading or listening to any of his books. I also went to his live chat in Glasgow which was very interesting and came away from it with a lot of practical thoughts for developing my own positive mindset. Over the years his books have definitely helped me with my issues, making it easier for me to navigate some of my own issues, and plan ahead with a more positive mindset.

Key points

- You don't need sugar, drugs, or social media. There are lots of positive things you can do to get the feelgood factor.
- Build in good habits throughout your day, and start with waking up in the right way – a bit of exercise, some fresh air, and good nutrition will set you up right.
- Stay active and get as much fresh air and natural light as you can throughout the day.

- Give meditation a go – it might not seem very easy to begin with, but stick with it and you'll find it's an excellent way to re-focus by soothing your mind and helping you let go of anxieties.
- Getting organised and finding a routine that works for you can take so much stress and uncertainty out of your daily life, helping you to seize the day.
- Put your trust in other people. Try and surround yourself with the right people – positive people – who will listen and help you in your life when you need it.
- Find inspiration, advice, and relatable stories in the books and podcasts of people you respect and admire.

Positive thoughts

- Don't be afraid to start all over again. You may like your new story better.
- Strong people don't put others down, they lift them up.
- People don't decide their future, people decide their habits and it's their habits that decide their future.

11. STOP GIVING A FUCK! DON'T LET YOURSELF BE CONTROLLED BY PEOPLE, MONEY OR PAST EXPERIENCES

You are the only person who has to live your life, do what you want, not what others tell you to do.

There are lots of good reasons why not giving a fuck is good for you. We all need to learn to relax, and try to adopt a more stress-free, zero-fucks-given lifestyle! But it's not always that easy if you're suffering from a mental health issue, particularly when your overactive mind spirals out of control. From primary school onwards, we all seem to be living more and more stressful lives. The pressures of modern living seem to be designed to hold us all back from living in a happy, stress-free way.

For some people, doubts about their own ability, appearance, worth and status can be crippling. You might recognise yourself in some or all of this list:

- If you fail at something, will you be embarrassed? Will you worry about what people will say?
- Do you ever feel that you are not good enough?

- Do other people's opinions hold you back from doing what you want to do?
- Do past decisions still eat you up?
- Are you trying to keep up with others' expectations?
- Are you worried that you're not fashionable enough or that your social media account isn't popular enough?
- Do you do things just to fit in?
- Have you ever thought, *Once I get this, I'll be happy?* Does that ever work?

Whatever it is you're not doing, or you are doing for the wrong reasons will only bring disappointment, regret, worry, and stress. We all need to learn to stop giving a fuck about others' input and opinions and do what we want, whether it's starting a new job, hobby or project. Stop worrying – stop people pleasing or trying to fit in – and start enjoying yourself.

Spreading payments. 'Ticked up' to the max, so many people these days live a life from month to month with all their money going to bills – to cover the costs of the big fancy house, expensive cars in the driveway and keeping up with the latest fashion. On their social media, they may look like they have the perfect life but really they're living month-to-month and worrying about covering their bills. As it is so easy to get absolutely anything on finance these days, it's very easy to start living out what you can't actually afford, causing stress and worry. A lot of times you'll hear people say things like, 'When I get this big house I'll be happy,' but the majority of the time they aren't happy, and they just end up struggling even more. You can't spend money to make your problems or your sadness disappear.

The fashion chasers you see online who buy expensive fashion to try to fit in, to impress, or to get those likes on social media may not even be able to afford what they're wearing. Especially at the time of writing, with energy costs and interest rates going up and up. There are a lot of people out there complaining about the rising costs who say they're really worried about how they're going to afford all their bills… walking about in £500 trainers. Obviously, if you're worrying about living costs you can't really afford the trainers, so why put yourself through all the worry and stress over a shitty pair of trainers that aren't even that nice? And the bigger question is: why do you give a fuck what other people think anyway?

By not giving a fuck about other people's opinions, their expectations and their fashion choices, and by doing what you want – and what you can afford – you will be a lot happier and less stressed, and you'll achieve more of the things you want to achieve instead of doing things to fit in, to impress other people or to pretend you're living a different life.

But what about the ways you let your own doubts and insecurities control you? How do you go about dealing with them?

Overthinking and self-sabotaging
Sometimes you're the biggest obstacle to your own happiness. Self-sabotaging is when people do – or don't do – things that block them from success or prevent them from accomplishing their goals.

Overthinking – or ruminating – is when you play things over endlessly in your mind. A certain amount of thinking through problems can be helpful. But overthinking and rumination are different: it could be that someone said something to you and it offended you. Instead of letting it go, you keep going over it in your mind, thinking about what you could have said, or what you should have done in response. You just can't let it go. One little thing can affect all sorts of daily tasks and long-term goals. Suppose that person said something to you at the gym; maybe you're so upset by it that you won't go back. That'll put an end to your exercise plans and will only make you feel worse about yourself in the long run.

Or it could be that you've got to face a difficult task – like going to get your teeth done! You're so worried about it, that you play it over and over in your mind. You fixate on all the things that could go wrong. By the time the appointment comes round, you feel like you've lived through the experience a hundred times and you're probably shitting yourself in anticipation of what's going to happen...

Sometimes these kinds of behaviours can actually lead you to cancel an important appointment. Every time you put something important off, or delay doing something that will help you feel good about yourself you're locking into the same bad behaviours and maintaining the cycle of depression.

Watch out for behaviours like:

- Avoidance
- Conflict
- Negative self-talk
- Procrastination

- Perfectionism

Driven by anxiety, fear, worry, and self-doubt these behaviours will affect your efforts to build the life that you want to live. The constant negative self-talk that makes you feel you're not good enough, and the excessive worry about other people's opinions will prevent you from achieving your dreams. Focus on a new hobby or project, reduce situations that can cause you to feel uneasy or worried and keep yourself in a positive mindset. Here are some ways to help you do that:

- Don't live a life you can't afford.
- Come off social media if it wastes too much of your time and upsets you or angers you.
- Stop comparing yourself to others and their achievements.
- Keep away from people that are negative and bring you down.
- Stop doing things to fit in and start socialising with people with similar interests.
- Focus on yourself and make small goals that you can work towards.
- Distract yourself. Read a book, go for a walk or listen to music. Do whatever it takes to take your mind off self-sabotaging talk.

As I said in chapter eight, you should learn to recognise negative thinking and identify the bad thoughts as they come into your head so you can challenge them. Don't give them a free pass to fuck up your day. Just recognise them for what they are and calmly and rationally dispute them.

Practise your own affirmations. What are the things that are good about you? What have you done today that proves you're working hard, being kind or making people happy? And if you can't manage that, start small: *Today I washed the dishes,* or *today I went outside.*

Keep a record of your achievements, including the small stuff, and refer to it when you need to fight back against your less helpful thoughts. You can even go back to remember things that you've achieved in the past so you build up a better (and fairer) picture of yourself and your self-worth than your unhelpful mind might like to paint for you.

Remember, there are real physical benefits to thinking more positively. Stress can have some nasty long-term effects on your body so the more you do to combat it, the better. But also, the more positive you are, the more likely you'll be to get out and engage with the world, exercise, see friends and family and try new things. All of that will boost your natural feel-good chemicals and stop you from indulging in bad food, excessive alcohol consumption and lazing around. It's a win-win.

Key points

- One of the most empowering things you can ever do is to stop giving a fuck about what anyone else thinks about you or the way you live your life!
- Rewrite the script on your own self-worth – you don't need anyone else's approval or permission to do the things you want to do.
- Don't feel pressured into spending money you haven't got to try and please people who don't matter.
- Learn to identify your own self-sabotaging behaviour, bit by bit. It can stop you from living the life you want.

- Learn to fight back by building up your own bank of things to feel good about.
- Remember that beating stress can actually make you feel healthier and happier.

Positive thoughts

- Stop buying things you don't need to impress people you don't like.
- You don't need a better phone, a bigger house or a nicer car - a better mindset will make you much happier.
- Everything that you are is enough.

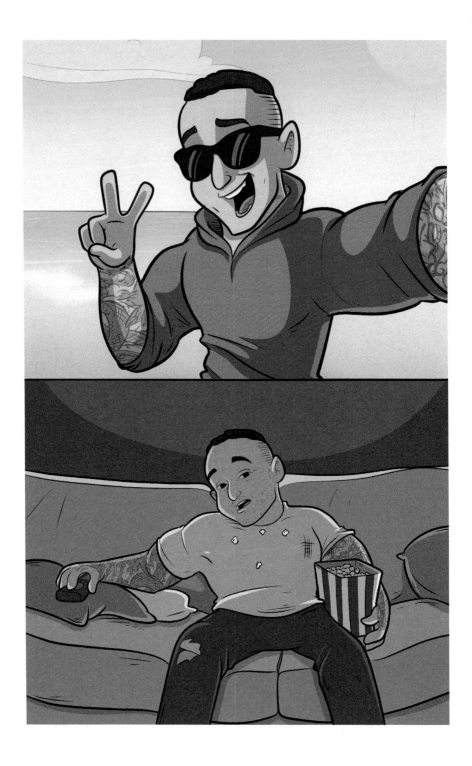

12. JONNY'S PROGRESS

Don't cry over the past, it's gone. Don't stress about the future, it hasn't arrived. Live in the present and make it beautiful.

As I write this, it's been about eight months since I was at my lowest ebb. I never ever would have imagined my life could get that bad and at its worst, I never thought I'd be able to drag myself out of the hole I got into. When I look back to the person I once was, I can see how panic attacks and anxiety crept up on me over so many years without me realising it. I still find it strange how much anxiety can affect you without you even noticing. Then when it gets to the point where you can't make excuses or block it out, it's very scary how much it fucks with your head. When everything fell to bits around the world in that bad year – and then that had a knock-on effect on my life – it obviously had a significant impact on my headspace. But I freely admit that my thoughts, emotions and daily decisions made it all a lot worse. If I had known the basics of mental health symptoms, and knew where and how to get help, I might have been able to make better daily choices that would have made a big difference when I was really struggling. If I had found help sooner, it might never have gotten to that point. I'm really hoping that some of this information will help you guys get a basic understanding of it all and hopefully help you start the process of helping yourself before it gets worse and spirals out of control.

My life has started to completely turn around now. Yes, I still have ongoing uncertainties in the outside world but I am not the same person I used to be on the inside. In fact, with the hard work and knowledge I've gathered, I am a much more positive, confident person. I'm happier and more motivated than before it all started to affect me. I feel I have a lot more focus, and self-direction; I don't worry about anyone's opinions, except the people I really trust and care about. I am enjoying living life in the present and setting goals for the future. Being in such a good place, with a much healthier, more positive mindset gives me the belief that I will never let myself get into such a position ever again. I am more prepared for anything now and better able to deal with difficulties if they enter my life.

Everything is on track now: my offshore work is busy and I am setting up another company that's started off very well and is picking up nicely. I have also been writing this book – it still shocks me when I think about that. Back in the day, I struggled to write a letter and now I'm writing a book! But those are the kinds of things that can happen when you remove the constant negativity and overthinking from your life. I have noticed that when you're in a negative mindset of fear, worry, and overthinking, you will only create more negativity and more problems. You will miss out on the opportunities that life offers you. But if you're positive, happy, and relaxed you will see possibilities and notice the opportunities coming to you. That saying: 'thoughts become things' has really stuck with me since I heard it right back when I started getting help. I really think hypnosis was the main factor in helping me to reprogramme my mind (alongside everything else I did). I have spoken to a lot of people about these issues and our various ways of coping with them and overcoming them and it seems that everyone has their own ways. You may find that it takes a bit of trial and error until you find what helps you best.

Looking back at everything that happened, if I had known what was actually happening to me, i.e., anxiety and panic attacks rather than physical health issues, and if I had known how to help myself, I wouldn't have needed the pills for my panic attacks. They were definitely a short-term fix. It still sounds so stupid that it took over my life so completely, but now I know all the bad things your mind can do if you let it; I just had to discover all the helpful, positive and empowering things my mind could do to fight back. For good and bad, your mind is the most powerful thing in your body and can completely change your life, one way or the other.

When this average Jonny took back control of his mind and made it work to his advantage the turnaround really was incredible. As I write this, I no longer suffer from any anxiety, and I have not had any panic attacks for years. The more I look for examples of situations that I went through with no worries at all the more I can find.

Flying on the helicopter to work and back ended up being my biggest problem as it was hard to distract myself when I was stuck in there for a long period of time with nothing to do, and no one to talk to (because of the noise). I now get on the chopper without having to take anything to calm me down, and I am sleeping before it takes off. Being able to drop off to sleep, without any anxiety shows just how relaxed I really am now.

Another decision I made recently really shows you how far I have come. I never liked the dentist. I had a few bad experiences and was a bit unlucky to have teeth that looked pretty shit – with fangs and other teeth going off in different directions. Your decision-making really suffers when you're suffering with anxiety, as you overthink everything and worry about doing something to the point where you just don't do it. I recently had a bit of free time and without thinking twice about it, I booked up to sort my teeth out. I flew abroad, was in and out of the clinic over the next five days, and got my whole mouth sorted, coming out with a shiny new smile. It's amazing just how easily I headed over there without overthinking it, and without worrying about looking like an international drug smuggler at the airport. At the clinic, I was calm. I didn't give a fuck about any of it, even though I needed about 50 injections in my gums throughout the week. Thank fuck it's done! I'm not going to lie, it was a pretty horrible process, but I'm really happy with the outcome, and I proved to myself how much I have changed.

So many day-to-day situations that would have pissed me off, or that I wouldn't have been able to get out of my head all day don't bother me now. I have noticed my temper is a lot better now, and I can take everything as it comes. I'm not just back to normal; I'm better than normal. 2022 was a pretty shite year for me and although, at the time of writing, it's only two months into the new year, everything is going so much better – it's going to be a fucking belter of a year!

Key points

- My story proves that anyone can take control of their mental health issues and turn their life around. If I could do it, you can too.
- I know that if I'd understood what was happening to me at the time – and if I had reached out for help sooner – I could have saved myself a lot of pain and anxiety.
- Things that used to make me anxious or might have brought on a panic attack in the past don't affect me any more.
- Even though I used to hate going to the dentist, I was able to overcome my fears and do it – and all because I have taken back control of my mind. Anxiety is not the boss of me!

Positive thoughts

- Whatever comes, let it come. What stays, let it stay. What goes, let it go.
- Tough times never last, but tough people do.
- We only have one life to live, so we have to live it the best we can.

Story Terrace

Printed in Great Britain
by Amazon

27062507R00071